SNAKES

# DEADLY VIPERS

**MONIKA DAVIES**

Gareth Stevens
PUBLISHING

Please visit our website, www.garethstevens.com. For a free color catalog of all our high-quality books, call toll free 1-800-542-2595 or fax 1-877-542-2596.

Library of Congress Cataloging-in-Publication Data
Names: Davies, Monika, author.
Title: Deadly vipers / Monika Davies.
Description: New York : Gareth Stevens Publishing, [2023] | Series: Deadly snakes | Includes index.
Identifiers: LCCN 2021050747 (print) | LCCN 2021050748 (ebook) | ISBN 9781538279922 (set) | ISBN 9781538279939 (library binding) | ISBN 9781538279915 (paperback) | ISBN 9781538279946 (ebook)
Subjects: LCSH: Viperidae–Juvenile literature. | Poisonous snakes–Juvenile literature.
Classification: LCC QL666.O69 D388 2023  (print) | LCC QL666.O69  (ebook) | DDC 597.96/3–dc23/eng/20211201
LC record available at https://lccn.loc.gov/2021050747
LC ebook record available at https://lccn.loc.gov/2021050748

First Edition

Portions of this work were originally authored by Dava Pressberg and published as *Vipers*. All new material this edition authored by Monika Davies.

Published in 2023 by
**Gareth Stevens Publishing**
29 E. 21st Street
New York, NY 10010

Designer: Sheryl Kober
Editor: Monika Davies

Photo credits: Cover, pp. 1, 5 Mark_Kostich/Shutterstock.com; cover (snake illustration) vinap/Shutterstock.com;  cover, pp. 1–24 (background texture) Anna Timoshenko/Shutterstock.com; pp. 1–24 (snakeskin) Natalliya85/Shutterstock.com; pp. 1–24 (halftone texture) MPFphotography/Shutterstock.com; pp. 3, 12, 19 (snake illustration) vinap/Shutterstock.com; pp. 4, 7. 8,  (fatal facts texture) Pakhnyushchy/Shutterstock.com; p. 6 Ondrej Prosicky/Shutterstock.com; pp. 9, 14 reptiles4all/Shutterstock.com; p. 10 Chief Design/Shutterstock.com; p. 13 Matteo photos/Shutterstock.com; p.16 Eric Isselee /Shutterstock.com; p. 17 frantic 18/Shutterstock.com; p. 18 Danny Ye/Shutterstock.com; p. 20 dwi putra stock/Shutterstock.com; p. 21 Jason Mintzer/Shutterstock.com;

Printed in the United States of America

CPSIA compliance information: Batch #CSGS23: For further information contact Gareth Stevens, New York, New York, at 1-800-542-2595.

# CONTENTS

Words in the glossary appear in **bold** type the first time they are used in the text.

# THE VENOMOUS VIPER

In a forest, a long and heavy snake waits calmly for its next meal. This snake's leaf-shaped head blends in with the forest floor. A rat runs in front of the snake, unaware of the nearby danger. Snap! The snake strikes, sinking its pointed teeth into the rat, **injecting** toxic **venom** into the small animal.

Meet the viper, a deadly predator that lives across the world. Known for their long, sharp teeth, vipers are a deadly type of snake.

## FATAL FACTS

Vipers are members of the snake family Viperidae. This big, wide-ranging family is made up of more than 200 species, or kinds, of different snakes!

Vipers are sometimes separated into two smaller groups: pit vipers and Old World vipers. Pit vipers have a heat-sensing organ, or body part, while most Old World vipers do not.

Vipers often come in colors that allow them to blend in with their surroundings. This is known as camouflage!

# SPY THE VIPER

With over 200 species, vipers come in all shapes and sizes. The longest pit vipers in the world are bushmasters. They can grow to more than 10 feet (3 m) long! Other vipers are less than 10 inches (25.4 cm) long.

Vipers come in many colors and patterns. The eastern diamondback rattlesnake might be gray or olive green with a diamond-shaped pattern down its back. White-lipped pit vipers are usually bright green but sometimes are blue. Copperheads are tan and rust-colored. Most vipers have triangle-shaped heads.

**FATAL FACTS**

One of the smallest vipers in the world is the Namaqua dwarf viper. It only grows to about 10 inches long (25.4 cm)!

# LIFE AS A VIPER

Most vipers are solo hunters and prefer to live alone. However, some, such as rattlesnakes, will sometimes share a den. Vipers do come together to **mate**.

Some snakes lay eggs, but most pit vipers give birth to live young. That means the mother viper doesn't lay eggs. She carries eggs inside her body, and her babies break out of the eggs before they are born. Some Old World vipers also give birth to live young, like the central Asian pit viper. Others do lay eggs.

## FATAL FACTS

All but one species of pit viper gives birth to live young. The bushmaster viper is the only pit viper that lays eggs when giving birth.

Vipers have a vertical pupil in their eyes. A pupil is the black part in the center of an eye that lets in light.

# WHERE COTTONMOUTHS LIVE

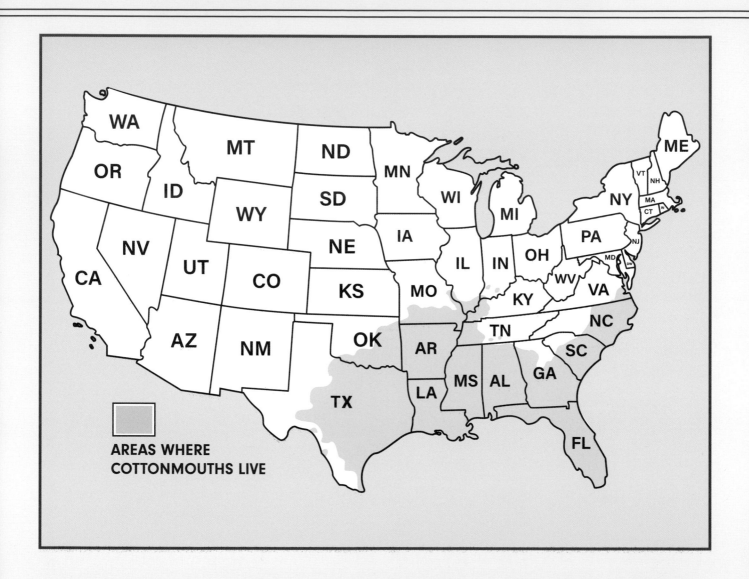

AREAS WHERE
COTTONMOUTHS LIVE

Cottonmouths are pit vipers found in the southeastern United States. They are often seen in swamps, or areas with trees that are covered with water at least part of the time.

# AROUND THE WORLD

Vipers live in a wide range of **habitats** and **regions** across the world. They are found in areas of North America and South America. Old World vipers live in Europe, Asia, and Africa.

The western rattlesnake lives across the western United States and in regions of Canada and Mexico. The bushmaster viper lives near the Amazon River. Many vipers live in trees. Rattlesnakes are found in dens during the winter. Some vipers, such as the cottonmouth, spend a lot of time in water.

## FATAL FACTS

Vipers can survive nearly anywhere and are found in deserts, fields, mountains, and rain forests. Some species prefer warmer areas, while others live in colder conditions.

# DEADLY SENSES

Like all snakes, vipers use their tongue to "taste" the air around them. They stick their tongue out to pick up certain smells in the air. Vipers then return their tongue to their mouth and pass the smells to a special body part called the Jacobson's organ. It's located at the top of their mouth, and this organ can recognize the smells.

Pit vipers also use their pit organs to sense heat from nearby animals. The pit organs are located between their eyes and nose.

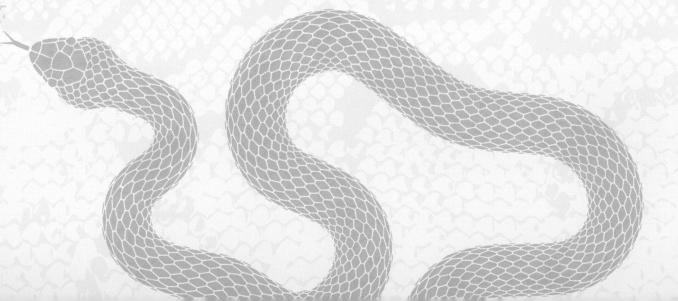

Pit vipers usually go out and hunt at night. Their ability to sense heat helps them find **prey** in the dark.

The Gaboon viper has the world's longest venomous fangs for a snake. This viper's fangs measure up to 2 inches (5.1 cm) long!

# A TOXIC BITE

Vipers are known for their deadly bite. These snakes are feared around the world because of their toxic venom.

A viper delivers its venomous bite with its fangs. Fangs are long, pointed teeth. They're sharp enough to break the skin of prey and then inject the viper's deadly venom. If a snake isn't biting prey, its fangs fold up inside its mouth. Some scientists believe adult vipers can control the amount of venom they want to use.

**FATAL FACTS**

One of the world's deadliest vipers is the saw-scaled viper found from North Africa to India. Some think this species is **responsible** for the most human deaths.

# WHAT'S FOR DINNER?

Vipers live all over the world. Since vipers live in many habitats, different species hunt different types of prey.

Many vipers eat whatever they can find, catch, and fit down their throat. They can stretch their jaws, or walls of their mouth, wide to swallow big meals. They often hunt small **mammals** found in their habitat, such as rats and mice. Some also catch birds and lizards. Vipers that spend a lot of time in water, such as cottonmouths, feed on fish and turtles.

All snakes, including vipers, are carnivores, or animals that eat meat.

Vipers prefer to stay hidden instead of moving quickly away if a predator is looking for them. But these "slow" snakes can strike with speed when they are hunting!

# ON THE HUNT

Snakes are skilled hunters with deadly senses. Some snakes called constrictors squeeze their prey to death. Vipers, on the other hand, don't always hold on to their prey.

Vipers like to strike and bite their prey, injecting their next meal with venom. They then often let it go to avoid the prey biting them. However, if their prey tries to run away, it quickly loses strength and often dies. A pit viper can then track their prey using its special sense of smell. Then, it swallows its meal whole!

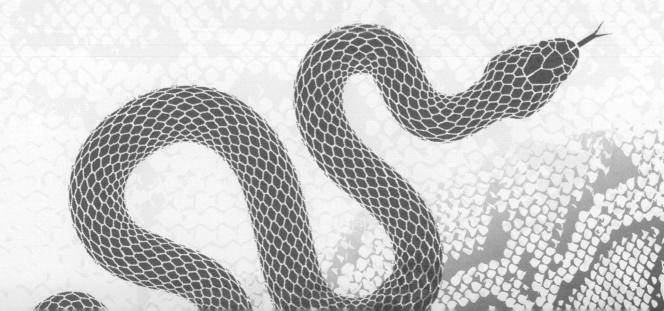

# CARING FOR THE VIPER

Some vipers, like the saw-scaled viper, are **aggressive**. Other vipers, like the Gaboon viper, are known for their calm and slow-moving nature. People are often afraid of vipers and their venomous bite. But humans are more dangerous to vipers than vipers are to people!

Some species of vipers are **endangered**. As cities grow and roads are built, vipers lose their habitats and homes. Vipers may have a deadly **reputation**—but they need our help to keep them safe.

Mangshan pit viper

The Mangshan pit viper and the Albany adder are two viper species that are in danger of dying out.

# GLOSSARY

**aggressive:** showing a readiness to attack

**endangered:** in danger of dying out

**habitat:** the natural place where an animal or plant lives

**inject:** to use sharp teeth to force venom into an animal's body

**mammal:** a warm-blooded animal that has a backbone and hair, breathes air, and feeds milk to its young

**mate:** to come together to make babies

**prey:** an animal that is hunted by other animals for food

**region:** a large area of land that has features that make it different from nearby areas of land

**reputation:** the views that are held about something or someone

**responsible:** used to describe a person or thing that causes something to happen

**venom:** something an animal makes in its body that can harm other animals. Venomous means able to produce a liquid called venom that is harmful to other animals.

# FOR MORE INFORMATION

## Books

Hirschmann, Kris. *Deadliest Snakes.* San Diego, CA: ReferencePoint Press, 2017.

Kim, Carol. *Pit Viper.* North Mankato, MN: Rourke Educational Media, 2019.

## Websites

### Awesome 8: Super Snakes

*kids.nationalgeographic.com/nature/article/super-snakes*
Read about more cool snakes on this website.

### Vipers

*www.dkfindout.com/us/animals-and-nature/reptiles/vipers/*
Find out fun facts about vipers here.

# INDEX